Refugees

A Chinese — Hawaiian Memior

by

Elizabeth B. Allbright

Refugees: A Chinese — Hawaiian Memoir

© Copyright 2016 by Elizabeth B. Allbright

Allbright, Elizabeth B., 1933-
Refugees: A Chinese-Hawaiian Memoir

Published by Mayeux Press
561 Bailey Drive, Denison TX 75091

These memories are dedicated to my grandchildren: Eva, Benjie, Lisë, Lillyann, Scott, Rosa and Isadora, and to my great-grandchildren.

My mother Betty and Me, Shanghai, Easter, 1934.

Table of Contents

Preface

November 10, 2006
Pine Lakes, Prescott, Arizona

   I have spilled these memories upon
these pages this past year because one
morning I awoke to the realization that I
am the only one left. No other family
members who took part in any of these
events are alive. I am seventy-three years
old now, so even the youngest Chinese, like
Ling, would now be quite ancient, if living.

Because of the truthfulness I feel I owe these people of beloved memory and spirit, I have made every effort to find evidence to support the factual framework of this history. Much of the memoir is, of course, colored by time and my maturity. I hope I have captured some of the raw perceptions of a young newcomer to this planet. Perhaps seeing war through the eyes of a child will awaken hope for peace among those who read this.

The battered and tattered pages of the big photo album are too delicate to flip about, so I have recorded on large file cards what is in the pictures. If anyone in the future wishes to research this history further, the cards may be of value to them.

It has been my good fortune to have talented friends and family to assist me in the writing of this memoir. My granddaughter Lise Jorgensen did a masterful job of editing. The first draft readers in Mexico, Gayle and Bob Rice; Jill Reinstatler; and Sandi Onsager gave me much needed feed-back. Annette Clift,

.

a new neighbor and friend formatted the pictures for me. My husband Paul gave continuous encouragement.

Thank you to all of you. And to my children Chris Crummett, Connie Jorgensen, Valerie Nelson, Andrew Crummett, Mary Page and Rob Crummett, I say, *These stories belong to you. They live in your DNA and the family culture. I am proud to bring them to remembrance for you and to share my life with you in these pages. Merry Christmas, and Happy New Year.*

L.E.A.

11

Chapter One

Shanghai Hai Tze

First Impressions

Picking at white painted iron, patting cool silk, and tickling the tissue curls that lined the bamboo arms of my baby cart are what I remember about being a baby. My small fingers became aware of the life outside my mother before taste, smell and seeing. In fact, "Bu yao doong tah" was the first command I was given in Chinese — "Don't touch!"

Memories of the other senses fixed themselves in my mind when I had grown enough to be aware of the play of opposites in my colorful birthplace: Shanghai, China in 1933.

I learned to tell the difference between a feral dog, or wonk, and a camel ambling down the street; between a flower and a blob of pink gum on the sidewalk; or between Peter Rabbit in my little picture book and a furry carcass lying on a work table in the kitchen.

Beautiful, shiny things in our home in Mimosa Court in the French concession, Tientsin, fascinated me. We had carved soapstone goddesses, tiny glass animals to put in the bottom of finger bowls, agate goldfish on table tops, and shiny brass fireplace tools to lure the inquisitive fingers of a child bent on discovery.

Very young children do not discern between themselves and those who take care of them. My mother seemed a part of me when she read to me at night. Amah too seemed an extension of me. She was my constant companion, washing and dressing me, and watching me when I played. Ling, our houseboy, often fed me and strolled about with me in his arms. Daily, they were my secure universe behind the gates of Mimosa Court.

Ling carried me clinging to his white linen jacket as he polished his way around the house. He smelled of soap and bleach and I sniff-kissed him on the neck to make him laugh. We would squat on the floor chirping Mandarin to each other as he polished the brass. I loved him dearly.

Amah slept in my room on a narrow cot and took care of me day and night. She was a tall woman from North China with bound feet only a few inches long. Her hair, pants and jacket were a gleaming black silk, smooth like all my favorite things. I absorbed many Chinese attitudes from her daily teaching.

I realize that this account, so far, does not mention my father. My first memory of him is so early in my life that it seems impossible. I sat up for the first time in the white iron crib. Two people came in to admire this event in my development. They leaned against the wall together and smiled. I usually saw them in a blur, in and out of my eating and sleeping, but this time they came into focus. It must have been early in January or February of 1934. I clearly remember, a long lifetime later, the sure impression that these two were my mother and father. I never again saw them as a couple. A few months later they separated and divorced after they registered my birth when I was eleven days old as an American Citizen on Oct. 12, 1933 with Washington D.C. The document is titled "Child Born Abroad of an American Father." They were divorced on August 12, 1935.

John and Betty

She was called Betty, but her formal name was Dorothy Elizabeth Raymond before she married John Carleton Myers. They met at a party in 1932 in Portland, Oregon. My grandfather, Ralph, and grandmother, Gezina, had settled in Portland after their glove factories had failed in Napa, California following the end of World War I.

Betty was born to what everyone thought would be a lifetime of comfort and plenty in Napa, but due to the vagaries of war, she was employed by Hills Brothers, the coffee company when John met her. She had a nice income and savings when many people in those depression times still were without work. The days when her father owned three glove manufacturing plants and managed hundreds of workers, the days when her mother could pay $100 for a plumed hat, were just a memory.

John was employed by a Portland newspaper. His father had been

Postmaster General in Portland, Oregon, and his mother, Lois, was a popular newspaper columnist. His good looks, charming personality and dashing role of reporter proved irresistible to Betty. Her slim figure and beautiful face, along with her bank account, were all John needed to prompt a proposal. He had an important assignment to cover the Japanese invasion of mainland China by way of Manchuria. It was exciting stuff, the kind of thing so glamorized in the motion pictures Betty loved. Convinced they were headed for exotic adventures, nothing that would risk life and limb of course, they bought steamship tickets. She was twenty-three years old, and he was twenty-six.

The wedding on December 13, 1932 was a modest one.

The *USS General Pershing* that would take them to China with fourteen other passengers was waiting at the dock. They left on December 28, 1932 and spent the long voyage to China doing what all honeymooners do. They partied and danced their way across the ocean to Yokohama, then Tokyo, then to Manila in the Philippines. There they transferred to the *General Sherman* and sailed on to Hong Kong. They arrived in Shanghai on February 28, 1933, after cocktailing and making love a quarter of the way around the planet for two months. The discovery that Betty was pregnant was a shock.

John immersed himself in the roller coaster ride of the newspaper business while Betty explored the streets and shops of the city. She took to carrying a sturdy walking stick because the beggars accosted her frequently. They saw she was pregnant and tried to touch her skirts with diseased hands, knowing she would pay to avoid them.

There were Chinese beggars in those days who had mutilated their own children to enable them to continue in the family business of begging. Some unfortunates had elephantiasis or as Betty would say, "God knows what all." She was kindhearted and gave them a few coppers before they got too close.

One of her first purchases in the city shops was a large bound book filled with heavy brown paper pages. Back in her cold, rented room, she arranged the high-backed chairs attempting to create a draft-free space. Then she enthusiastically filled the album with notes, photos and menus from the ship.

John was a photographer as well as a reporter. Some of my earliest pictures show me as an infant sitting in his camera box. Photography must have been difficult in those days with unreliable film and processing. Nevertheless, he took some remarkable pictures. His eye for detail and his interest in the common laborer's lives are evident in some of his best work. I have some small photos of Chinese street life that must have been sent to Betty's parents before they came to China. My grandmother put them in the back pages of a small leather covered album.

Many of Betty's photos of them together, or of John alone are missing. Betty must have destroyed them in her disappointment and despair, but I have three photos of my father. One is of him riding in a rickshaw, another is a head and shoulders shot, and the last is of him with his pals at the newspaper. I believe he was of slender build, average height, with curly dark hair and a high forehead. My mother always said he had beautiful legs. He was the surviving member of a pair of twins, and probably was pampered and treasured as a baby. He had three brothers: Frank Stott Myers, Jr., Raleigh Stott Myers, and Robert Leland Myers. Thanks to my cousin Perrin Smith, whose mother Mary Laura was my father's sister, I also have a photo of the four brothers taken in Portland in 1921.

John's penchant for drinking with his colleagues in Shanghai became a problem early on when Betty found herself with me in her arms, locked out of their hotel room due to failure on

John's part to pay the hotel bill. Betty's whole steamer trunk filled with her carefully chosen trousseau was to be held for nonpayment. This became a pattern in their lives. John would always apologize, and try to make things right by borrowing money, but eventually, his alcoholic nature was the undoing of their marriage.

Papa And Nana

I was born in a charity hospital in Shanghai, China on October 1, 1933. John was there and held my mother's hand. My doctor was a Canadian man who had a baby boy a few months old. His son's outgrown clothes were handed down to me. My mother told me that she had only one baby bottle and a couple of shirts for me, but she had diapers that had to be washed in the bathtub by Wong, a servant she had acquired who was devoted to us both. I was known among the Chinese as a Shanghai *hai-tze*, or a Shanghai baby. To my family, I was always Betsy because I am an Elizabeth like my mother.

Wong loved to make chocolate fudge for my mother. She once told me that she ate a whole pan of it everyday before I was born. Perhaps due to my mother's chocolate diet before I was born, I was an odd little baby, weighing only five pounds at birth. One of my eyes refused to open for weeks, and my pictures show that I had a problem with my tongue wanting to peep out between my lips. If I ever smiled, it is not evident in my early pictures. But my mother loved me, and so did my grandparents who had read between the lines of my mother's letters and had recognized her unspoken cry for help. They sold or gave away all their furniture, including a grand piano, and sailed to China to rescue their darling Betty.

My grandparents were married in Napa, California on February 20, 1905 when the century was new. In 1933, Ralph and Gezina Raymond were fifty-

one and forty-eight years old,
respectively. The adventurous spirit that
took them to Tahiti when they were
younger was still alive when they took
up residence in the Krier Hotel, Tientsin,
China. A couple years later, I was fed
delicious German chocolate pudding that
the Kriers cooked whenever they knew I
was coming to visit.

Bapa, as I called him, found a job
soon after their arrival in China. My
grandfather Ralph was a talented and
resourceful man whose ability to make
the best of a situation would be of
service to us all throughout his life. He
was always my hero. I know he was
devoted to my mother and to me. His
love affair with my grandmother lasted
his whole life from the time he met and
married her.

Nana, as I called Gezina, was an
orphan who was raised by her older half-
sister. Born in Marysville, California,
Gezina Gherkin was educated by nuns
in Benicia, California. The nuns saw her

musical talent and gave her lessons. After Gezina married, she played the piano with verve and gusto for many of Ralph's entertainments in Napa; her fingers raced over the keys playing both popular and classical music. When they met, Ralph was smitten by Gezina's looks and personality. A beautiful young woman with white blond hair who modeled in prim European costumes for a female photographer, Gezina was probably California's first pin-up girl. The framed and delicately tinted pictures were hung in homes throughout California. There is a story about how Ralph felt about her modeling career after they were married. When an ambitious photographer in town set in his display window an enlarged picture of Gezina that Ralph had taken of her sitting by a stream surrounded by wild flowers, Ralph stomped into the photographer's place of business and demanded that he take the photo out of the window. Nobody was going to put his wife on display.

Though he was wiser and mellower a quarter of a century later, Bapa was a man of strong opinions. My grandfather always read the English language newspapers carefully whenever he could get them in China, looking for trends. He was alarmed by England's weakness and inability to see the Germans' huge appetite for other countries. I was born when Adolph Hitler had been appointed German Chancellor, Franklin D. Roosevelt was president of the United States; and when Cordell Hull, who played an important role in our family history, was named Secretary of State.

Tientsin — Betty And Richard

The reasons for the move to Tientsin are unclear. However, my mother did everything she could to become independent and able to support me on her own. She lived in an apartment at first where she borrowed a typewriter, found a book on shorthand,

and practiced until she felt she was good enough to get a job as a stenographer. Soon she was hired by A.M. Karagheusian Rug Company. The company was owned by Armenians who hired Chinese to manufacture oriental rugs. They styled themselves as a *Tientsin-American Corporation for Overseas*. They dyed their own wool yarns and created their own patterns, weaving them on huge looms. Betty made friends with the staff. Among them was Arthur Richard Archibald Boycott, known as Richard, who was in charge of the dyeing process.

The first home I can remember is the one on Mimosa Court. Our neighbors there were the British Boycotts, Richard's family. His father was a university professor of mathematics; and his mother owned a small knitting factory. Their sons Richard, Teddy and Michael lived with their parents in the family home.

My mother dated Teddy and others

in the heady social life of the European-Americans in China. There was a French naval officer named Jacques-Yves Cousteau who was much taken with my mother, but when he found out that she had a child and was divorced, his staunch Catholic upbringing cooled his ardor. Many years later he became world famous with his work in undersea exploration.

Eventually, Richard Boycott's fine qualities won my mother and they were engaged in April of 1936. They were married and honeymooned in June, 1936. Their marriage document lists her as a stenographer. My two grandfathers, T.A. Boycott, and R.J. Raymond were witnesses. Their wedding portrait shows my mother dressed simply but stylishly in white, with Richard dressed in a white linen suit. She looks confident with a small smile, while he looks very nervous and distracted. She told me many years later that she was quite surprised and a little disappointed on the morning after their wedding to discover Richard preparing for his usual ball game with the boys.

Born in Birmingham, England, Richard was very active in sports: ice hockey, polo, and swimming. I once heard him tell of saving a Chinese man who was drowning in the river. When he had pumped the water out of the man, the man told him, "You are now responsible for my life, and therefore have to support me for the rest of it." Richard, who spoke Mandarin Chinese fluently, refused the offer, but gave the still dripping fellow enough money to fill his rice bowl for a long time.

In many of those early pictures Richard looks rather solemn, but he was really a very amusing person with funny stories about his days at an English "public" school where he was sent at the age of six. The boys were housed at the school without central heating. Richard was so cold that he learned to tuck his ears inside the ear canal to keep them warm. This habit broke down the cartilage in his ears and gave them a "cauliflower ear" look. He was a small wiry man, no bigger than my mother, with a handsome face and light brown wavy hair. Having spent most of his life in China, he was very comfortable with his Chinese friends and enjoyed playing their drinking games with them. I have pictures of him doing the table banging game; he is beaming with happiness and pleasure.

During the Tientsin years, the name of Chiang Kai-shek came up often in conversation between the servants. He sounded like a hero who was going to make everything better for the Chinese. Of course, if they said so, then I believed it. There was something, too, about soldiers who were brave, and Japanese who might shoot us. I kept these ideas in my mind.

Chapter Two
Here Come The Japanese!

It was not long before tensions
began to build in our home. War nerves
and apprehensions of what might happen
gave the adults white knuckles. I know
now that my mother was trying to work
while bullets bounced off the outer walls of
her office. My daddy Richard was going
around wearing a uniform and a scowl. I
knew he had a gun that he was supposed to
use if the Japanese came. Unlike children
of today, I had no idea what a gun could
do, but one day standing by the window in
the second floor bedroom of our house, I
saw hundreds of soldiers marching down

the street. They were nearing the entrance to Mimosa Court. I yelled as loud as I could, "Daddy, Daddy, get your gun, here come the Japanese!" Immediately, Ling cupped his hand over my mouth and pulled me away from the window. The Japanese had invaded Tientsin. Nothing would ever be the same again.

In later years, my mother said that the Japanese troops had been wading through mud and were very short on rations, so short that they attacked living cattle on the road and tried to butcher them for food on the spot.

Our big album shows newspaper pictures of civilian war dead rolled up in front of the rubble of crushed houses. Titled "Hostilities in China," we saw photos of dead children and horses. Those images filled me with a deep sense of badness, a gut-rumbling wrongness that has stayed with me all my life. Over the years, every war increases that feeling.

There were also photos titled "At

Nankai University" showing piles of rubble
and trashed books, a smashed street lamp
and wrecked buildings. I wonder now if
that is where my Grandfather Boycott
taught.

Them And Us

Sand bag barriers were set up on the
boundaries of the British Concession on
Woodrow Wilson Street outside Krier's
Hotel with soldiers guarding the area near
the river. Bapa took me to see it all and
pointed out floating bodies in the muddy
water. Lacking understanding of what it
all meant, I was stunned and wondered
why nobody was trying to rescue the
people floating by. If my grandparents had
any inkling of how horrified I was, they
didn't show it. We have a picture of Nana
chatting with a soldier while Bapa and I
stand still for the camera in front of the
sand bags.

One of the unexpected bits of
wisdom I received from this study of

pictures, written comments by my mother, and old memories put into modern context is this: people, nice people like my family, had an attitude of "them and us" that we have been working to eliminate for the past seventy years. They seemed to view other races as objects, rather than as brothers and sisters. The British "stiff upper lip" and "empire" spilled over to the Americans in China, but the Americans had a stiff shot of arrogance all of their own. Respect for the regular Chinese person was weak. On the other hand, I think that it worked both ways. One of my early memories is of standing by the imposing gated entrance to Mimosa Court, looking through the wrought iron and watching a Chinese girl carrying her little brother on her back. She was close enough to talk to, so I politely asked in Chinese if I could come out and play with her. Whether from fear or disdain, she wrinkled up her face at me and spat out that a person like me was not anybody she wanted to play with. She turned her back and stomped away. It seemed to me that the baby on her back looked at me with cold eyes. The fact is, both of us had been told by our respective parents that our playing together was forbidden. But at age four, rules like that didn't make any sense to me.

Another time, I was walking along a street with Amah where we could see a platform in the middle of an intersection. A very tall, dark man with cloth wound around his head and white gloves on his hands was waving his arms around, directing traffic. He interested me, so I began asking Amah questions. She shushed me up immediately, and told me never to look at those men on platforms because they were bad and would give me the evil eye, maybe even steal me. No nice lecture explaining, "the policeman is your friend." The Indian Punjabi towering above us was alien in her eyes, therefore dangerous.

The Chinese in our house at Mimosa Court were always kind and loving to me. Yong, the cook, made me a special one egg custard every day called "softa pudding." Amah made me little embroidered slippers with bug-eyed dragons on them. Ling told me to eat my slightly burned toast because it would make me have nice white teeth and curly hair. Of course, that was a joke because I already had curly hair. I know now that Ling and Amah had trouble in their lives. Ling's wife had a baby girl that they could not afford to feed. He told my mother to her horror that they had to "Shrow her away." He cried when he said it. As for Amah, except for her tiny bound feet that pained her, I have no idea of her life, or her problems. Neither of them ever gave me any hint of their difficulties, wanting me to be happy. And I was, most of the time.

Bound Feet And Other Shocks

One day, Amah, probably in a playful mood, pretended that she was going to bind my feet. Now, I had seen her feet every night when she re-bandaged them. I had seen the toes curled like fists around the soles; I had observed the peeling skin and misshapen ugliness that

hid under her black satin slippers. I knew
that her feet always hurt and that she
couldn't walk very fast or run.

   As Amah unwound a roll of gauze
bandage tightly binding my toes, I
struggled to get away. I was horrified that
she wanted to do such a mean thing to me.
Terror pushed screams out of my mouth
and tears ran down my face.

   "Amah!" She who had always been
gentle and loving was trying to hurt me! I
slapped at her hands; I would have kicked
her if my mother had not burst in to rescue
me.

   That trauma, so innocently
conceived by Amah when I was three years
old, was an early lesson in never taking
anyone for granted. My guilt at having
slapped and yelled at Amah was part of the
terror of the event. We had always been
respectful of each other. Respect, or "face"
is an integral part of Chinese relationships;
each of us had lost face in that experience.
I know now that tiny feet were a mark of

beauty to women of her class. The incredibly minute size was achieved by years of suffering. In her mind, perhaps, she really did want me to have what she considered an asset, a mark of beauty. Neither of us knew how to retrieve our old balance in the relationship after that. Face was a power to be reckoned with.

To maintain face, my mother entertained as did all her friends in the community of *China-hands* as non-Chinese Americans or Europeans were called. Nobody had the full complement of serving dishes and glassware for a crowd, so there was much running back and forth by the servants, borrowing this and that from the neighbors. Alcohol was the major ingredient required for having a successful party. As a baby, I was in the habit of drinking my water from a barrel shaped shot glass. At one party, I could just see over the edge of the table where I spied my little glass. I was thirsty, so without a word to anyone, I grabbed my little glass full of what I thought was water and gulped it down. My mother says that I landed on my bottom with a very surprised look on my face--the glass had been full of gin. There was a big to-do with everyone feeling guilty and I was bundled off evidently undamaged.

Another story about parties involves a hostess who was a new arrival to China. Even though it was winter, everyone at the party was impressed with her abundant supply of ice for drinks until a curious guest found out that she had sent her "boy" off to cut some ice out of the pond for the party. The guests tried not to gag and began to worry about their digestion because the pond was a receptacle for sewage during other times of the year.

China fooled everybody occasionally. One afternoon, when I played in the neighborhood playground alone, a powerful sand storm swept into Mimosa Court from the Gobi Desert without warning. It slammed me face down then covered me with waves of choking sand and dust. Wind-blown particles blinded me as I tried to sit up to call for help. But the wind was too strong. The dust and sand were in my eyes, nose and mouth. Suddenly, help came. Strong hands grasped me by the shoulders and swung me up and out of the sand that was beginning to bury me. A wooly shawl was wrapped around my head by a neighbor who had been looking out her window. She rushed me to the arms of my family. That experience taught me respect for weather, and for the kindness of strangers.

Chapter Three
Refugees

The days in Mimosa Court were coming to a close. No more elegant parties or trips to the Forbidden City for Mom or "horse hockey" or fishing with me at Peitaiho for Daddy. No more afternoons with Amah at my side while pink blossoms like ballerinas dropped from the Mimosa trees. Nana had wired her sister Elizabeth Langer in San Francisco to tell her of the conditions in Tientsin. Elizabeth then wired the State Department in Washington D.C. to inform them that an American family was stuck in the midst of the war between China and Japan. A wire was sent by Cordell Hull, Secretary of State, to the authorities in Tientsin that the Raymond and Boycott families must have passage arranged for them on the first available transport.

These are my mother's notes regarding the leaving of China due to the invasion of Tientsin:

"Left Tientsin October 22, 1937 on a special train under Marine guard to Chingwantao. Took from 11:15 a.m. to 2:15 a.m. to make trip.[1] Boarded U. S. Destroyer *John D. Edwards* at Chingwantao and the quarters were crowded. Were treated royally. Had navy beans for Saturday lunch.

"Reached Cheefoo 12 hours later at 2:00 PM and were transferred in small boats to transport *Chaumont*. Left Cheefoo at 4:30 p.m. for Yokohama [Japan]. Very crowded on *Chaumont* with refugees from

---

[1] This wartime trip took fifteen hours.

Shanghai and Tsingtao. Reached Yokohama 9:00 A.M. October 27, 1937. Stayed on board until arrival of *President Hoover* at 10:30 PM. Sailed at 9:30 A.M., November 2. Arrived Honolulu, November 9, 1937 at 8:30 AM."

Memories of that evacuation come in stress-filled images for me: we said goodbye to China and my Chinese family of Amah, Ling and Yong; I hugged Daddy who had to stay behind. We rode on the train with armed soldiers posted outside on the steps to the doors. I was frightened by their presence so I wanted to pull an emergency cord to stop the train. I was scolded for trying. At night, struggling to sleep in a hammock aboard the destroyer with my mother beside me, we watched a puddle spread over our heads as someone above wet the hammock above us. I remember sitting on a bench at table with the bread in paper wrappers and milk in cans. Since I was used to a "Downton Abbey" style of service, I had never seen food offered that way.

As my mother notes, we crossed on a floating ramp from the destroyer *Chaumont* at night to board the *President Hoover*, a passenger ship. In my mind's eye, I can still see the flickering electric lights on the water in the port of Yokohama. We had to walk unsteadily on a shifting temporary bridge over the black and tossing ocean. All of these impressions formed a lasting dislike for the word "refugee."

Honolulu, Oahu, Territory of Hawaii

Our trunks had been packed for San Francisco. Nana was looking forward to seeing her sister and nephews, and my mother was ready for the protection of the United States, but that was not to be. Bapa was an adventurous fellow and loved new challenges. He had arranged to meet some business friends when we docked at the port of Honolulu on our way to San Francisco. They met him in a long touring car at the dock and proceeded to give him a ride around the island with, I assume, a running commentary on the advantages to settling there. They offered him an interesting, well-paying job with American Factors, one of the "big four" companies in Honolulu. I think I heard Nana reminding him that he was not the one who would have to set up housekeeping until the trunks were delivered months later.

When he returned draped in flower leis, after being wined and dined in one of the best restaurants, he said to me, "Come on *Shmaltz*, we're getting off here. This island is beautiful and I've got a good job here!"

I was glad to give up my hobby of cutting out pictures in magazines and pasting them in a book. My mother had got me started doing that during the hours of the voyage when I was alone in the cabin. Instead of making up stories about paper people, I was going to have another real adventure. As for the trunks, well, they would have to go to San Francisco by themselves, as Bapa said, then turn around and sail back to Honolulu some time in the future.

The four of us found an apartment a few blocks from the beach and settled down. I spent my first night sleeping on a narrow sofa in the living room with chairs lined up next to it to prevent me from rolling off. One night, I woke up from being chased by a fiery dream dragon. Responding to my frightened sobbing, my family found me underneath the chairs, none of which had moved. Nobody could figure it out, least of all me.

The apartment was on the second floor. There was a long flight of wooden stairs outside the back door which led to a small back yard. I claimed the shady space under those stairs as a place to play. My toys were in the trunks which had sailed away, so I asked for a carpenter set with a hammer, saw and nails. My Bapa bought a child's starter set and I set to work making little things in my own way which turned out to be much harder than I expected. Betty Boop, my favorite doll, was soon forgotten and my Noah's ark was a vague memory. Nana had given me a piece of a white fur collar that she had worn in China and it was my most prized possession. That and my small swan's down pillow named Bydi, "soft white" in Chinese, were something to pet when things got confusing. In later years, I named several cats Bydi.

Language Difficulties

One of the big adjustments that I faced as a bilingual child was that there was nobody to speak Chinese to. Even the Chinese people who ran restaurants in Honolulu spoke a very different dialect. My daddy was still in China fighting the Japanese and he was the only one in the family who knew how to speak Mandarin Chinese. In Tientsin, my mother and grandmother often called upon me to translate, and bargain for them when we shopped. My mother and Nana knew a few words, but not enough to carry on a conversation. So I made a decision in my childish mind that in this new country,

I had to speak English only and to speak Mandarin Chinese was unacceptable, rude somehow. So I stopped thinking in Chinese.

There is a funny story about how I was already trying to get this language difference figured out when I was about three years old. A visitor to our home noticed that I had gotten quite dirty playing outside and said, "My dear, it looks as if you need a bath." The lady was British, so she pronounced bath with an "ah" in the middle: *bahth*. I looked at her in surprise and explained, "Oh, no! Boys take *bahths*, and girls take baths." I said this because, of course, that is how my two parents pronounced the word according to their British and American accents. In Hawaii, when I began school, there was a new language to learn, pidgin.

A big Hawaiian house with its accompanying army of termites became available to rent. It had a veranda with French doors across the face of it and big airy rooms with hardwood floors. My room was large with plenty of space to set up a doll house and toy shelves. There was a wide front lawn with very tall coconut trees, hibiscus and other tropical plants, a sandy back yard with more hibiscus and clotheslines. My grandparents had a large screen porch for a bedroom, and when Daddy came back, my parents had their own wing with bedroom, sitting room, and small bathroom. Our living room and dining room were large and soon were furnished in rattan furniture with colorful cushions and an oval dining table with enough chairs for the whole family and guests. The best part was that we were one block closer to Kuhio Beach on Kalakowa Avenue.

I liked living in a real neighborhood with Hawaiian people living near by. All we needed was a pet.

Armed with my ideas about language and its appropriateness, I went to call on a Hawaiian family down the street. I was about six years old, but had mastered the local pidgin language. I knocked on the door of an older boy named George who had shown me his kittens in a coconut palm hat to ask if I might have one or two. His big Hawaiian mama answered the door. Looking up respectfully at her round brown face I made my pitch in pidgin. There was a silence. She drew herself up to her full rotund six foot one, and peered down at me and boomed, "Hey, you! Haole girl! How come you talk like that? Why you no talk good English?"

Sizzling with embarrassment, I held back tears as I started over in proper polite English. I really wanted to run away, but I held on. It seemed a matter of huge importance, as if I were speaking for my race. Besides, I had never had a kitten, and this was my big chance. She listened intently and then smiled. "You go pick out two good ones. Is okay wid me and George." She even let me use George's hat when I promised to return it after I had taken two orange and cream kittens home. I hoped that Daddy would like them when he came to Honolulu.

Daddy finally arrived and we went to meet him at the dock. There are pictures of that day, as well as a picture of him on shipboard with other refugees from China. In that picture, he is standing with his arm around a very pretty blond woman. There are big smiles on both their faces. You get a feeling that they have had a fun-filled, special time together. Looking at it as a mature woman some seventy seven years later, I would say that he had a fling for himself. Richard did not look very happy to be back with us, at first.

When Daddy discovered that I would not speak Chinese to him, he was very disappointed. Sadly, I absolutely refused. I said in a schoolteacher voice, "Daddy, we are here now where they do not speak Chinese. You have to speak only English." I guess it was the only way I had to keep the two parts of my history separate. The change was so drastic, from Mimosa Court with Ling and Amah to Honolulu where we were on our own, where my mother and grandmother had to do all the cooking and housework. I couldn't keep my balance, even at five years old unless I embraced the new life with my whole heart.

Daddy was a survivor, though. He set up a little lab in their studio wing where he studied electronics. He made a little radio, using instructions in some books he sent for. He also set up a dark room for processing film. Meanwhile, he looked for work. His experience as an expert in rug making did not translate in Honolulu, but his interest in electronics did. Pearl Harbor needed him so he learned on the job and became a master electrician, working in the dry docks and on ships. The rough men he met there called him "Limey." They didn't know at first what to make of this English gentleman, but they found out he could do the work, and so he found his place with them.

One day, many months after he arrived in Honolulu, a surprise was delivered from a recently docked ship to my mother. It was a large camphor wood chest, beautifully carved. In it was a complete set for twelve made of bone China--everything including egg cups. The whole set was decorated with hand-painted gold and brown bamboo. It was a magnificent gift that he had arranged for before he left China. Due to the war, it had taken almost a year to get to my mother.

A Queen's Bowl And Breakfast With Bapa

I enrolled in St. Augustine's, a Catholic school, which my parents chose because I didn't have to cross any streets to get there. The nuns were of the Maryknoll order. My kindergarten teacher was Sister Agnes; she taught me and the other children who were from the streets of Honolulu how to sing French songs, make paper chains, and plant seeds. During playtime, we scrambled around in a giant banyan tree playing a silly game called "Pick-a-Lock." Our kindergarten graduation picture was taken in front of that wonderful tree.

One day when I came to school on a
Saturday to play on the swings, Sister
Agnes had a little talk with me about God.
I think I must have told her that I wanted
to be a nun, and that my parents were not
Catholic, but Episcopalian. She explained
that it did not matter where I was; I could
talk to God. She said, "You don't have to
be in church, but can even be in the sand
pile and talk to God." It was not long after
that the bishop came to visit St.
Augustine's. There was a grand procession
into the church, and a Hawaiian girl and I
were selected to sprinkle flower petals in
the bishop's path. The honor embarrassed
me because I felt I didn't deserve it; after
all I was not a Catholic yet. Every night I
prayed that my parents would let me be
one.

During that period, Bapa made
many friends in the business world. One
day he brought some Hawaiians home to
meet us. Bapa arrived carrying a small
wooden bowl that they had given him. He
explained that it was a poi bowl that had
belonged to Queen Wilhelmina of Hawaii.

He wrote a history of the bowl on a piece of paper and stuck it inside, but sadly over time, the paper disintegrated. We visited the Queen's home once as tourists and saw the very large wide bed that had been hers. It was called a *pune*, pronounced "poonay." It became common for people to have a pune in their living rooms when I was growing up on Oahu. It was a sort of lounging spot, big enough for several people and served as a guest bed, too.

We were living a good life there at 147 Kealohalani Street. Bapa and I would get up early on Sunday mornings and make our own breakfast. Often we would go a few blocks over from our house to Aioki's, a store owned by a Japanese family. Mr. Aioki would cut us a piece of sharp Tillamook cheese, or wrap up some bacon or smelly Limburger for us to take home after Bapa had paid. Bapa would make himself coffee, while I would have a special drink. It was a hot coffee flavored drink called Postum. It had no caffeine because my grandmother believed it would stunt my growth. Sometimes after breakfast, we would walk down to the beach again, and he would watch while I splashed around in the waves or picked up shells. Afterward, I would get sprayed off with the warm, rubbery-smelling water from the garden hose to get rid of the sand and salt. My sun suit would just dry on me. Nobody cared if I wore the suit for days because it got washed that way almost every day.

Raymond family, Napa - Ralph, Gezina, Betty

John C. Myers, 1932

Sampan owner,
Whangpoo River,
Photo by John C.
Myers

Passport Photo,
1934

Richard & Betty,
wedding, June 1936

Richard and Chinese friends

My Amah

Ling Fu Shen & me,
Mimosa Court

Nana, me at one
year, and Joe P.
Joe, our rickshaw
man

Me, age four

Refugees, Bapa, Mom, me,
aboard the *President Hoover*

Oahu, at the beach

Our house on Kealohalani Ave, 1941

Aunt Molly, Uncle Seth & Tammy Dog

Enthusiastic beachcomber, 1941

Haena Dr, Manoa, off to school with gas mask

At Castles' home above Kaimuki, Palolo Valley

Mom & I on Christening day, Aunt Molly behind me, Uncle Seth sitting

Our Christmas party during the war

Mom & I leave for California, Jan, 1946

Chapter Four
Pearl Harbor Attacked

One Sunday, Nana had made a big breakfast for the adults, but I was next door playing dolls and reading funny books with my friend Mary Jean Waite. Mary Jean had a Hawaiian grandmother and a Danish grandfather so her hair was almost white blond. She was my best friend. We were both startled when we heard the dinner bell Nana always rang to call me, and then we heard my mother actually screaming my name, to come home right away. This had never happened before. As I have written in my poem about December 7th, *Pearl Harbor*, this was a day

that changed our comfortable, easy-going
aloha lives forever. As I ran up the three
steps to our lanai, I could hear the radio
voice of someone sobbing. A grown man
crying! I heard the words: "Our island has
been attacked by the Japanese!" It was the
governor of Hawaii on the radio.

Phones rang, and then the President
all the way in Washington D.C. came on
the radio. Daddy dressed to go to Pearl
Harbor. The day seemed to crackle with
an electric tension, but it also felt heavy
and scary to my young mind. Planes were
shooting at each other over our house. A
bomb dropped on the other side of the
block near my school, but none of the
Japanese occupants were home. My
mother later wrote that doors up and down
the street were slamming as men in
uniform rushed to get to Pearl Harbor.
Daddy was picked up down on Kalakowa
Avenue by a fellow worker.

Here is the poem I wrote about that
morning. I was a student at Mills College

at the time. It was published in "Walrus" in 1988:

Pearl Harbor

Sunday morning, Honolulu,
lying on my back
skinny knees propping up the funnies,
I hear the grownups stir
Kona coffee and sugar in their cups
Papaya boats lie empty on their plates.

My dad, his hair curly-wet
from the shower answers the ringing phone,
runs to change into his electrician's clothes.
Nana blows her nose,
snatches up the big black lunch pail
scalds coffee, squashes tuna sandwiches together.
My grandpa rushes swearing out to the street.
"Stay inside," he yells, "stay inside."

Behind a rattan chair I watch
my grandpa in the street. His voice
mix-mutters with neighbor men who stand,
a knot of chins pointing up
feet shifting weight, twiddling pocket change
while in the sky small planes play tag
over our roof.

My mom is thin in white shorts,

white mouth and eyes,
I want to hug her, but
She's pulled too tight like
a wire I must not touch.

They let me walk out to the sidewalk;
we wave goodbye to Dad.
He carries his lunch pail,
his hair Vitalis slick,
walking in big work boots
down the leafy street away from us.
We watch till he gets small.
My grandpa pounds the map
on the dining room wall,
dropping bright pins and flags.
I don't know why he hates the Japanese.

Nana packs his mainland clothes in the steamer
trunk.
I don't know when they will come back.
Before he leaves, Grandpa comes
down the hall in the blackout
with a flashlight to chase away
the spiders who want to make
a tent over my bed.

When Daddy comes back from Pearl Harbor,
he talks about dry docks, salvage, cranes,
the duration, bomb shelters,
gas masks, war.
He jumps when coconuts fall on the lawn.

My grandparents had to evacuate Oahu. After we had all been given identification cards the authorities were able to identify the residents of Hawaii who needed to be sent to the States, or Mainland as we called the U.S. Since they were in their fifties and not employed by war effort jobs, Bapa and Nana were chosen to leave. They found safety in Northern California far from danger in a place called Grizzly Flats. I was told that my grand father got a job there as a caretaker.

We had all been issued identification cards on May 28, 1942, at least that is the date on mine. It seems rather a long time from December 7, 1941, to be doing that, but perhaps the date on mine refers to the inoculations I was given for typhus and other diseases of wartime. My skinny little fingerprints are on my card in addition to an identifying mark: "small dent on forehead." I had walked into the corner of a table as a baby in China and dented my skull. It also mentions that I had been issued a gas mask. No mistake, we were at war.[2]

Haena Drive

Both my parents were judged to be essential to the war effort. My mother worked for a "big four" firm called Alexander and Baldwin. While our Waikiki beach had already become a maze of barbed wire, and after Mr. Aioki's store changed its name to something patriotic, we moved to the mountains of Manoa above the city into a house perched on top of a hill on Haena Drive. The rented house had a screen porch entry, living room, two bedrooms, a bath room, kitchen and back porch. The basement, big enough to walk around in, became a shop for Dad.

---

[2] "The attack on Pearl Harbor claimed 2,403 lives and left 1,178 wounded. As well, 19 American ships were damaged or sunk and 149 planes lost..." *Eye Witness To The American West*, by David Colbert, Pantheon, 1997.

Mom set to work making heavy black drapes for the windows to comply with the island blackout laws. Our neighbors, the Sanders, outfitted their garage which was built into the side of a hill as a bomb shelter for themselves and us. We spent many a tense hour with them while search lights lit the skies during air raids. The Sanders had an interesting house, a big orange dog named Taffy, and goldfish in a vase hanging over an indoor grotto. Paul and Eleanor Sanders were a brother and sister pair who taught music at the University of Hawaii. One room of their house was taken up with twin grand pianos. The Sanders interested me in the arts; they took me to concerts and plays where I saw world-famous actors like Boris Karloff and musicians who came to Hawaii to entertain the troops. They introduced me to Joe Rosenthal, the famous photographer who later took the photo of the Marines raising the flag on Mt. Suribachi, Iwo Jima.

Our lives in Manoa changed in some way almost every day. When we were issued our gas masks, we found that they weighed eight pounds and had to be worn whenever we were away from home. Mine hung from my right shoulder on a strap which crossed my torso. The mask banged on my left hip as I walked. My growing body compensated by making my hip more padded on the left than on the right.

My dad was assigned to the graveyard shift at Pearl Harbor. As a result, I hardly ever saw him, but on Sundays we went to St. Clements Episcopal Church where I studied the lives of saints in Sunday school. Once during a service, I sat next to Admiral Chester Nimitz, Commander of the Pacific Fleet, dressed in his white dress uniform covered with medals. He was aware of my awe and turned his head to smile at me, and in that moment, I knew that we were in this war together and both needed God to get through it.

I was enrolled in a school owned by the University of Hawaii that was within walking distance, although I had to toil up and down several nearly vertical hills. It was part of a teachers' college, so we were subjected to all of the newest theories on teaching. We had a supervisor, who was an experienced teacher, and two student teachers who happened to be of Japanese descent.

At this school, emphasis was on teamwork, especially in sports. I had never been interested in competition, liking to swing and play in sand or on bars at my Catholic school. Before we moved, I had a few months at Thomas Jefferson School. All I can remember about that is that we were encouraged to help the war effort by collecting tin foil. Aluminum foil had not yet been invented. We students tried to produce the biggest tin foil ball in the school. The foil came from gum wrappers and candy bars. Some months later Mary Jean and I had a bout of home schooling which Mom and Mrs. Waite had organized, but that too had never involved anything more athletic than hopscotch. A miserable round of being picked last was my lot at Teacher's College School followed by embarrassments, and loss of face for running the wrong way in football, missing catches and pitches.

About this time we heard from my grandparents, the Boycotts. They had tried to escape the war by leaving from Manila in the Philippines, but the Japanese captured them and put them in concentration camp at Santo Tomas. The buildings of a university there had been turned into prisons. My grandfather was lucky in that he was put in charge of the library. My grandmother Boycott busied herself knitting socks from every little piece of string and thread that unraveled from the old clothing of the prisoners. Their youngest son Michael was incarcerated also. As the war went on, their plight there became more and more dangerous and we heard nothing.

My life at school was not all bad. We did some colorful wall murals about insect life, and learned to raise and mount butterflies. I loved reading and writing, and because English was spoken in my home and books were plentiful there, I excelled. This did not make me popular. My worst enemies were the Portuguese kids. I think now that they felt inferior to the bright Asian kids, and they didn't have the respect that the Hawaiian kids received, so they picked on we few *haoles*. In addition to me there were two white boys, and one other white girl named Laurel. Since the three other *haoles* were good at sports, that left me as the scapegoat. My teachers fell into the general mood of "let's pick on Betsy." They would talk about me in Japanese, making the other Japanese kids laugh.

One day at circle when the class discussed the news of the day, I told everyone about my grandparents' incarceration at Santo Tomas. That did it. My two young teachers were embarrassed and probably felt some guilt for the war, so I was persona non grata from then on. I was called names like *chimerinner*. It took me years to figure out what that meant. (I'm aware now that it meant that I interrupted too often, a common trait in my family.)

After Patsy Esperanto, one of the biggest Portuguese girls, took off her shoe and began to pound me on the head with it on the playground, the situation came to a halt. The supervisor finally stepped in. I think my mother may have had something to do with it.

The Caissons Go Rolling Along

The whole school met every morning in the gym to hear a pep talk from the principal, and to sing patriotic songs. I still know all the words to the theme songs of each branch of military service. My favorite was the Marine Hymn. Music was not the big part of life that it is now for young people. We didn't have any actually, unless our parents bought records and played them. Mine liked classical music so it swam through the air on weekends. For me, classical music was synonymous with happiness and security.

When we were told at our morning assembly that we were going to have a school band, we kids could hardly contain ourselves. Real instruments had been donated for us to use, and we could choose which ever one we wanted to play. I signed up for the drums. I have written a short story about that incident which was published in a collection at Berkeley, California, years later.[3] But the upshot of the school band story is that I was told that "girls do not play drums." Now, I only had a snare drum in mind when I signed up, but perhaps they thought I meant a bass drum. I have no idea now what went through their heads, but I ended up with a flute. Most of my girl pals had clarinets. The music instructor was a young service man on loan. He had never played the flute. He was much more interested in teaching the boys to play brass instruments anyhow. Needless

[3] The short story, *For The Duration*, is included in the Addendum of this book, page 125.

to say, I was a reluctant musician. The Sanders tried to interest me in the flute, bless them, but even after they took me to hear a professional play in concert I couldn't stick with it. I wanted rhythm.

One of my last memories of that school was April 12, 1945. I was allowed to stay after school to finish painting my section of a mural when our supervisor, Miss Trout, came into the room with tears in her eyes. "The president has died," she said. "President Roosevelt died today." I was stunned. He had been president for my whole life. He was like a member of the family. We listened to his radio fireside talks and felt he was keeping us safe in the war. My eyes still sting when I think of how much he meant to everyone on the island, and to me.

Aunt Molly And Uncle Seth

One bright spot in those years was my "Aunt" Molly and "Uncle" Seth. Molly had been a schoolmate of my dad's in

China. He discovered her by chance in a
Waikiki restaurant one evening just before
the war. Aunt Molly was auburn haired
and freckled, fine boned and lovely. Tall
with slicked back black hair, Uncle Seth
Castle had been a cowboy in the western
U.S. and had traveled extensively in
China and Manchuria. He was an
importer-exporter of Chinese artifacts.
The Castles lived in a huge rented estate
at Waimanalo Beach right on the ocean. I
spent many heavenly weekends with
them, playing on the surf-torn rocks of the
jetty, climbing the plumeria trees, making
leis, and helping Molly in the kitchen.
They had a dog named Tammy, a little
Scotch terrier who thought he was my
older brother. Molly always wore white
silky clothing that gave her a peaceful and
angelic look. However, her passion was
animal rights. In those days she had no
organizations to join, so she talked to me
instead about her disdain for zoos and the
crime of hunting wild animals for sport.
She would sweep her black oriental carpet
with damp tea leaves carrying on a
convincing argument against using

animals for tests while I sat on my haunches and nodded. My very Chinese habit of squatting and silently nodding had become a part of my young personality.

Making Friends With The Enemy

After December 7th, at our home on Kealohalani, the Japanese workers who were a part of our lives continued to show up regularly, but they no longer chatted at the kitchen door. The man who picked up kitchen scraps for his pigs still arrived with his big square tin cans, and the man who snipped the edges of our lawns with scissors silently did his work, but I couldn't get him to talk to me any more.

When we had moved up to Manoa, the only Japanese we knew were Maki and Sian. Maki was the maid in the Shanahan household a few blocks away on Lanihuli Street. She vacuumed the fuzzy white rugs, and polished the silver service, mopped up, and occasionally cooked for Inez Shanahan. Inez was married to Doc Shanahan, a chiropodist who is featured in my story "The Seed Business."

The Shanahans had three children I played with every day: Patty, Mike, and Colleen. They seemed incomparably wealthy because there were hundreds of comic books scattered around their play room. "Sheena of the Jungle" was my favorite. The family always kept a big bunch of bananas hanging in the basement for us kids to eat, and there was a large rubber tree to climb. Avocado, trees tall as California oaks, dropped their fruit on the lawn in season for the cats and hungry boys and girls to eat. The crowning treasure was a small merry-go-round in the back garden. When I saw it for the first time, I told myself that I must memorize it so that I could tell my children someday.

The Shanahans' big sloping lawn behind their house ended at an alley which led to the neighborhood tennis club. Maki and Sian lived behind the tennis clubhouse in a dwelling made of loose bricks, boards and other cast off materials. You had to crawl or be sitting down to keep from bumping your head on the ceiling. Around this place were vegetable gardens, flower gardens and odd items that I didn't question, not wanting to be rude. On her bed, Maki had a carved wooden block for a pillow. She cooked over a fire at her home, I think, but I only saw her cooking in Inez's kitchen. Maki was famous for her semoy, a pickled prune treat, and her vanilla ice cubes. She was always nice to me and treated me like one of the family.

I never saw Sian in the Shanahan's sumptuous home, but his kingdom was the tennis court. He took care of it, along with the rackets, net and balls, and the changing room where the neighbor men showered. He was really only about thirteen, but seemed adult to me. We never talked about the war or anything much, but he did speak English. His backhand was as strong as any man's. I

loved to watch him play tennis with the
club members. If he went to school, I
didn't know about it.

Mom Goes to Kula Sanatorium

Aunt Molly and the Shanahans
became much more important to me after
the Public Health people came to the
school to give us little x-rays to check for
tuberculosis. Mine had some spots on it,
so they told us to come down to the bigger
x-ray machine in Honolulu. My mother
took some time off from work to take me.
When my film was read, it showed that I
had fought off tuberculosis and formed
calcified spots where the disease had
lodged in my lungs. The technician was
explaining this to my mother, who was her
usual charming self. As a way of flirting
with her, the technician idly suggested that
he take her x-ray. When the film was
read, our lives were once again shaken to
the roots. My mother had active
tuberculosis. She had to go to a hospital

on the island of Hawaii, a place called Kula Sanatorium.

It was April. Aunt Molly taught me to make a little yarn chick. Dad and the Castles stood with me in a circle around my lei-draped mother to say goodbye. It must have been at an airport. I handed her the chick and kissed her. She was so thin I could feel her ribs as I hugged her. Everything felt dark and heavy, except that I was going to be living with the Shanahans. Fate had made a choice for me. Since my mother told me she couldn't give me any brothers and sisters, especially older ones, I was disappointed. Now I was going to get a family of brother and sisters to live with while my mother was away.

Mom stayed at Kula for nine months. She almost lost her life there when her lungs filled up with liquid, but she survived with good care, fresh food raised right on the hills surrounding the hospital, and clean, cool mountain air.

My mother's letters to friends in the U.S. prior to this experience reflected a cavalier lack of respect for people of color. It was considered smart and witty to refer to Asians as "slant eyes," and Hawaiians as "dark meat." This sounds outrageous now, but that was the war talking. My mother was cured of that attitude when she roomed with women of all races at the hospital. Her best friends were Japanese and Hawaiian women there. I never heard her use ugly terms describing people of different races again.

During her stay in the hospital, my dad was working seven nights a week at Pearl Harbor. So I went to stay with Aunt Molly and Uncle Seth after a case of food poisoning had nearly killed me at the Shanahans. It was not anyone's fault but mine; I had opened an exotic, but very old, can of mushrooms and heated them when Inez was sick. Nobody else ate them but me. The Shanahans, especially Doc, were quite upset, but Aunt Molly and my mother from her bed at Kula, insisted after the food poisoning episode, that I live under the watchful eyes of the of Castles.

Molly and Seth Castle now lived in a house on Wilhelmina Drive above Palolo Valley and the town of Kaimuki. Like us, they had moved as far from the beaches as possible to be safe from enemy attack. Their house had a glass porch that overlooked Palolo Valley where we could see tiny figures walking in the streets around the small houses below. In the morning we could hear the roosters down there welcoming the sun at dawn.

The garden at my new home was rocky, so we only had a few plants in cans. My favorite was a succulent that had little pale green puffy bell-like flowers. New plants would grow from the notches in the leaves. Another plant was called Jobe's tears. It produced silvery gray bead-like seeds that could be made into necklaces.

My bedroom was an attic room at the top of a flight of stairs that Molly called "the wooden hill." An ancient Chinese bronze squatted on top of the

cupboard at the head of the stairs. It had
been dug up by an archeologist. I
imagined it was buried with a little
Imperial princess who had died young.

Molly had wonderful antique
Chinese furniture and carpets. The living
room was dominated by an ornately
carved ebony table. It was so tall. I could
rest my chin on it. It had bowed legs and
probably weighed more than 400 pounds.
Another antique was a screen with scenes
embellished with semi-precious stones.
Cranes flew across it with ruby eyes and
pearl wings.

Uncle Seth drove me to my new
school every day and I rode the bus home.
It was a city school named for Robert
Louis Stevenson. I felt lost in such a big
school, lost and bored because my little
school had taught me so well that I was
ahead of my peers there. I missed the
Shanahans, roller skating in the garage to
records of the *Sons of the Pioneers*, our tree
climbing and playing pirates. I missed
their avocado trees and working to rake

the Chinese grass for pocket money from Doc.

I used those earnings to buy equipment for my chemistry set from stores in downtown Honolulu. I'd wait at a bus stop and soon a nice person would offer to drive me to town. Once, a chauffeur-driven car pulled up to the bus stop for me. I was driven in a car fit for a queen. It was the team spirit, *the aloha way* to help others. That generous spirit was one of the few good things about wartime.

I was living with the Castles when I experienced my surfboard epiphany. Somebody had given me a huge redwood surfboard. It was heavy and long and more appropriate for a six- footer than me. Just the same, I was proud of it. I'd wait at the Surf Rider Club where it was propped against the wall a few yards from the water until a biggish boy or man came along. He would carry it for me down to the shallows. From there, I'd ferry it, pushing and swimming with one arm until I was out where the waves in glass-clear arches marched toward me in the moderate surf.

One day I wanted to try bigger waves, so I maneuvered my big old board to a spot out by the reef. Sun umbrellas on the beach were tiny colored dots, but nobody under them watched me. I was by myself having bussed down from Wilhelmina Heights. The water sloshed gently against the wooden board as I waited for a wave. One came, but my timing was off. As I launched myself onto the board, the wave hit in such a way that my board flipped up and banged me in the back of the head. I slowly sank down through the sun streaked water, but the wave's momentum was not through with me yet. It slammed me against the coral reef.

Calm, deep and lazy, took over. I felt no pain. My open eyes watched seaweed drift by. Bubbles followed me as I sank down, down to the peaceful sand where I wanted to sleep for a while. There was no fear, no time, just sweet peace.

Then someone spoke to me saying, "You have a choice. You can stay here, or you can work to get to the surface." These words appeared in my mind, as whispers of golden sunlight streaming down through the dark water.

Like the obedient child I was, I cared about the voice. I wanted to please it. I knew what it wanted me to do. I willed my muscles to comply. There was no adrenaline rush, or clawing to survive-- just methodically pumping limbs. I was a strong swimmer, but I was gasping when I surfaced to see my board bobbing away in the distance. But with the vagaries of the sea, it was washed back in my direction. I grasped it and rested my cheek on my old wooden friend. Remembering the face-down deadman's float my dad had taught me, I finally felt my board scraping the sand. Somebody dragged it back to its place at the wall, and I brushed the water and sand off and caught the bus to Kaimuki.

Aunt Molly thought I was malingering when I complained the next day about my neck hurting. My arms were not working right either, but she made me do my laundry by hand in the wash trays outside as I always did on Fridays. Pain and outrage! Oh, well. I didn't tell her about my accident, because then she might not let me go surfing again!

My cervical spine injury had life-long effects that showed up when I was an adolescent, and later as an adult. But stiff necks and headaches were a small price to pay for the certainty that there was and is a protector and comforter always with me--one who will guide me no matter what happens.

I was growing up. People began to compliment me on my hair. Those were the days of Shirley Temple and sausage curls. My hair fell easily into curls like hers. There were always enlisted men and officers around the Castles' home on weekends. One of them was a fiercely

mustachioed man called Red who claimed
to have been one of first Marines on the
beach at Tarawa, in the Gilbert Islands.
We won that bloody battle in 1943.

There was another visitor, a soldier
who had been a hair dresser in New York.
He said he loved my hair and talked about
it too much. He brought me a baby doll
as a gift. I was ten, and baby dolls had
never been terribly important to me,
especially new ones. I had had my
favorite ones when I was little. Liking any
new one would seem disloyal to my old
ones. There was something about him
that Molly and Seth did not like very
much either. He never came around again.

Holidays Without Mom

My Aunt Molly suffered from
anemia. Our Christmas preparations were
too much for her, so Uncle Seth stuffed
my stocking and generally took care of
things. My dad was able to come to their
house for Christmas. He brought me a

whole set of doll furniture. Poor man, he tried to do the mom things; I didn't have any small dolls to use the furniture at Aunt Molly's, but he didn't know that. They were packed away in my old room at home. He had fixed a beautiful Christmas stocking for my mother filled with wrapped gifts and was going to fly there for a day with her. I knew why I couldn't go, but it hurt me a bit.

Uncle Seth gave me about a dozen Zane Gray Western novels, and several novelty pins made of coconut shell and tinsel. I loved the grown-up novels, and have had a "thing" for cowboys all my life.

Aunt Molly had found me a special model doll made of wood that you could make clothes for. She was a shaped like a woman, not a child. Along with her came a sewing kit, so we set to work making a wardrobe for my lady. Aunt Molly specialized in very tiny stitches like her amah had taught her, so that was what I was supposed to learn as well. I did my best, even learned to make flat folded seams and hems on the model's tiny, stylish outfits.

My mother had always been skilled at designing and sewing clothes for me and my *Storybook* dolls. These were a commercial line of porcelain dolls about six to eight inches tall that were dressed to be characters in classic children's stories. I had a nice collection of them with beautiful extra costumes that both my mother and Aunt Molly made for them. Two of my favorite costumes that she made for them were a "Gone with the Wind" outfit, and a Carmen Miranda costume complete with the turban covered with tiny fruits and flowers. I think that one of these was a gift for when I had my tonsils out while we were living on Kealohalani. I had been diagnosed with malnutrition, which I found faintly insulting. I liked being skinny.

The doctors must have thought that my chronic sore throats had something to do with the malnutrition and swollen tonsils. The operation, which is frowned on by doctors today, was supposed to get rid of my persistent throat problem. Children were operated on as if tonsils were not supposed to be in one's body. Adults had the same thing happen to them with appendixes. Nevertheless, I finally began to gain weight after the surgery and so my mother made me some new clothes to fit the new me. She would see a pretty dress or sun suit in a magazine or in a department store window, then would buy the material and copy it. I was always very proud of my mother's skill and usually loved everything she made.

Mom made me a hand tooled leather coin purse with my name on it in her handicraft class at the hospital. It was my most treasured possession, but somebody stole it when I swam at the YWCA. I must have gotten a free bus ride home because I had no bus tokens. Tears come to my eyes even now when I think of that loss. I missed my mother terribly when she was at Kula, but like my longing for China, I tucked the pain back to where it was safe—back to where I did not take it out and look at it too often.

The day finally arrived when my mother was well enough to be released. I was there at the airport to greet her, I'm sure, but strangely I have no memory of that event. I think now that I was so shocked to see my mother so changed that it was as though she were somebody else pretending to be her. She was very pale-- no tan at all. And she was fat. That took some getting used to. Being in bed for nine months and being urged to eat to survive had changed her. Luckily, children adapt quickly, so I was able to get used to having my mom home, but not working. She had to rest most of the time, so she dressed in elegantly long hostess gowns and rested on the *pune.*

During that period she wrote a story about me and a bunch of imaginary characters called *blums* and *mulbs.* I have it still. She also painted some wonderful pictures of scenes from Revelation in the Bible. They were fabulous in my eyes.

She had once been commissioned to draw the illustrations for a book about Hawaiian *menehune*. They are the small people who are said to have built the fish ponds and grottoes in the islands. When she was doing research for the drawings, the author took us to a cave near a blowhole where a giant was supposed to have sat. We saw the imprint of his enormous behind on the floor of the cave. Sadly, the author backed out of the agreement later. I thought that my mom's pictures were mysterious and wonderful. My favorite was of the mermaids combing their hair, while the *menehune* crouched on the reef watching them.

Aloha Hospitality

My mother gained her figure and her strength back. We began to entertain service men again. The war in the Pacific brought young men from their Iowa farms, from their apartments in New York, from the beaches of Oregon and the small towns all over the United States to

Honolulu where they were sorted out and sent to duck bullets, bombs, bayonets and torpedoes in some heaving ocean or on a strange island they had never heard of.

They were young, socially inexperienced and home sick. The USO people knew this so they organized dances in the evenings at the Banyan Court, at the Royal Hawaiian Hotel by the sea. There were two hotels in Waikiki at that time: the square white Moana and the pink Royal Hawaiian. My mother dressed up and did her patriotic bit by dancing with those young men dressed in their most formal uniforms.

So far from home, facing an uncertain future, they covered their fear with bravado. The young servicemen would walk four abreast on the narrow sidewalks of Waikiki on purpose to confuse a young woman coming in the other direction. I often stepped into the gutter to avoid them. They would roar around in their jeeps, hooting and whistling at girls. At twelve, I really

didn't know what it was all about. But
there were a few very nice gentlemen,
usually non-commissioned officers who
took me out for lunch with my parents'
permission. We sat at linen-covered
round tables overlooking the beach, and
chatting about sisters or horses back
home. They were honorable men who
enjoyed the company of a young person
who was interested in their life back
home. I think of them fondly to this day.

Life in Honolulu during that period
was not always polite and mannerly.
Racial slurs against the Japanese were
scrawled on public walls. Fierce Uncle
Sam popped up on signs everywhere with
slogans like "Loose lips sink ships!" The
capital V with three dots and a dash could
be seen everywhere. It was Morse code
for the letter V for victory. I think the
"Kilroy Was Here" cartoon started to be
seen drawn on walls and sidewalks then.
But the old Hawaii could still be glimpsed
in front of the hotels where the majestic
old Hawaiian women sold leis. They
dressed in muumuus or *holukus* and wore

large palm leaf hats adorned with flowers and feather hat bands. The carnation, plumeria, or pikake leis were draped over their plump brown arms as they called out, "Flars, flars!" The sailors in spotless white, their round hats on the backs of their heads, drifted in bunches admiring the younger women who bustled by them smiling secret smiles. The fragrance of flowers blended with the appetizing smell of teriyaki and saimin cooking in tiny improvised kitchens curbside, while the shaved ice man added his cries to the babble, and other men lurked in dark doorways beckoning.

Of course now, I understand much more about what was going on than I did then. I realize that contact with civilians kept the young service men anchored in reality. My mother and dad invited them home for drinks and home cooked hospitality in the spirit of aloha. What we cooked was dependent upon what we could find in the stores, or what the little vegetable truck would bring by once a week. Sometimes the vegetable man had fresh caught fish, but often we enjoyed steaks that had been smuggled under the officer's blouses when the military cooks were not looking. Meat for civilians was rationed.

In the long blackout, the men who couldn't pull themselves away in time for curfew stretched out on our cool, hardwood floors with lounge chair pillows and talked into the small hours.

Near the end of the war, we began to get visitors who had survived battles. My bed- room was right next to the living room, so I heard them telling their stories. One redheaded sailor named Joe had been on a bombed ship that turned into a fireball. He jumped into the oily sea, but the sea caught fire too. He floated in and out of the blazes, hanging onto a piece of wreckage until he was saved. He told us that night at our home that he was due to ship out again. Telling his story worked him up so much that his anger and fear boiled out in tears. "I don't want to die," he kept crying. The other men did what they could to comfort and reassure him, but I lay on the other side of the wall paralyzed with helplessness.

Sunset Days

Our days at Haena Drive were coming to a close. Daddy had adopted me in August, 1944. My mother and I were christened in the Episcopal Church. On that day, Aunt Molly and Uncle Seth officially became my godparents. The war was over, thanks to God's grace and the sacrifice of millions. My own experience with the ending of the war is reflected in my story, "The Effigy in My Closet" published by the Scribblers, in Napa, California in a collection titled *More Than Wine.*[4]

General Douglas MacArthur and his forces recaptured the South West Pacific. My Boycott grandparents and

---

[4] *The Effigy In My Closet* is included in the Addendum of this book, page 117.

Uncle Michael were saved from sure
death the day before the Japanese pulled
out of the Philippines. Japan surrendered
after our devastating bombing of
Hiroshima and Nagasaki August 6 and
August 9 and World War II ended on
August 14, 1945. War dead were
estimated at 35 million, with more than 10
million in concentration camps. Peace
with Japan was signed aboard the USS
Missouri with General MacArthur present.
We have a photo of that momentous
moment that was published around the
world. All Americans alive then felt we
were there on that deck too.

The end of the war meant that we
could obtain passage to the United States.
It was a sort of lottery, I believe, with my
parents waiting patiently for a phone call
to tell us when there would be space for us
on a ship. Commercial air travel was not a
possibility those days. The *China Clipper*
delivered mail to the islands before the
war, but that beautiful white plane had
disappeared from the skies. During the
war, only military flew overhead. If we

spotted a strange plane, we would quickly squint to see if it sported a star on its wing.

For me, California was a sort of magical, peaceful place where, as my Nana said, "Roses bloom right next to the sidewalk." With all of the glorious flowers of Hawaii for me to love, roses had become the most desirable because they couldn't bloom in the islands. Seeing my Nana and Bapa again was another dream to come true in California. They had settled again in Napa, and would be waiting for us there.

Getting ready for the move was complicated by the fact that we had no winter clothes. My mother rounded up some coats from people who still had them and we put together some outfits that would not look too "gawky" to the sophisticated San Franciscans when our ship pulled into port.

While the packing and sewing was going on, my dad prepared a cat mansion for our Ling. Ling was a Siamese whose beauty had not been spoiled by wedge-head breeding. He bossed the household, as any smart cat is bound to do. The authorities said we could take him to the states, but he would have to go ahead of us on a different kind of ship. He had to have a special wooden crate with drawers for his food and potty pan, as well as little ladders inside for exercise. A platform near the top was where he would rest and peer out. Daddy spent hours building this crate. He put Ling into it every day to get him used to it. He would talk to him man to cat, about what the trip would be like and about the people who would take care of him.

On the day when Ling was to be driven in his crate down to the dock, Dad called him to his cat breakfast. No cat. We called and searched. No cat. I was getting frantic because I had to leave for school, when our neighbor across the street called. She said that Ling was lying on her *lanai*. He looked very peaceful and relaxed, but he was dead. When my parents examined him, there was no sign of illness or injury. We talked to a doctor about it who said that perhaps Ling just didn't want to leave his home.

The ship we were assigned to was an Alaskan liner which had been designed to navigate narrow passages through icebergs. It had been turned into a small battle ship with heavy artillery on top. Needless to say, it was going to have a rough time in the great swells of the Pacific Ocean.

We boarded the ship, my mother and I, with high hopes and trepidation. Daddy stood on the dock waving, as did many of our friends. His job at Pearl Harbor would keep him there for a few more months. As the ship began to move away from the dock, all the passengers threw their leis into the water where they floated like a flower path back to my beloved island.

We had to share a tiny cabin with a stranger. I had the top bunk. I amused

myself by climbing up and down. After
we were under way, we were served hot
dogs and beans with sauerkraut, American
treats that we had not had in wartime. We
all ate heartily, and afterwards went to our
cabins for a rest from all the excitement.
It was not long before everyone on board
became seasick, even the crew. The ship
doctor was overwhelmed. All he had to
offer us in the way of "medicine" was a
stash of oyster crackers.

After a few days of thinking we
were going to die, I was the first to get my
sea legs. I wandered around the ship,
noticing that there were a number of
people who seemed to have no cabins to
sleep in. They were draped all over the
sofas and lounge chairs in the various
parlors in various positions of despair.
Sea sickness can make the most optimistic
person wish for a swift end to existence.
When it went on for days, some people
tried to medicate with alcohol with dire
results. But nothing was so miserable as
the fate that awaited a young woman

onboard who developed a severe case of appendicitis.

Nothing could keep the sick and dizzy passengers from staggering to a spot on the deck to view the dramatic arrival of an ambulance pontoon plane that was supposed to land on the sea and take the ailing girl and her mother to a hospital on the mainland. Far below us, her small lifeboat bobbed in the shifting, dark water. We could see her lying on a stretcher covered in a white blanket. The wait was prolonged, probably because our cracker-peddling doctor got his wires crossed about the arrangements. Finally, we saw the white plane of mercy, with big red crosses on its wings, flying low, coming in for a landing on the surface of the frigid water. We all clapped for encouragement.

But somehow, it was not meant to be. The plane nosedived into the water, the wings broke off and the pilots and nurses floated in the water hanging on to orange life jackets. They climbed up rope ladders that were provided by our ship's crew. The girl and her mother were hauled aboard, too. We heard the next day that our ship rendezvoused at night with a ship equipped with an operating room and surgeon.

Our ship continued its journey to California accompanied by leaping dolphins who flashed their silver smiles. We arrived in San Francisco Bay early one morning in January, 1946. I was amazed at the chill fog, but thrilled at the sight of dry land. The Golden Gate Bridge glowed with the sunrise, setting a misty stage for the next chapter of our lives.

We were met by Bapa and Nana who drove us to Napa. We stayed with them in their rented apartment at first. I was in the seventh grade at Napa High School. Due to a shortage of school buildings, we who were actually junior high age shared the old high school with the older students.

My homeroom teacher was Miss
Mehl. When she introduced me to my new
schoolmates, she said that she had climbed
trees with my grandfather as a schoolgirl.
I didn't know whether I should be
embarrassed, or proud. I decided to be
proud.

My first American flower friends
were freesias, daphne, and of course,
roses. My first experience of them was
when I walked to school on crisp
mornings and peered into the gardens I
passed. I sniffed their fragrance, so
different in a colder climate, and touched
their petals with reverence. It comforted
me that God made flowers for different
climates all over the world. California did
not have umbrella-like trees like the
Sanders' golden shower with branches
spread as wide as a parking lot, or torch
ginger in shadowy corners, or rubber trees
made for climbing children. California's
gifts were in sweeping rows of grapevines
or in tiny bright wild- flowers.
Nevertheless, I dreamed of Hawaii every

night until I saw it again, eleven years later.

In those first months, I met the children of my mother's friends. I taught them to hula, and they taught me many things about being a teenager, but that is another story that leads to many new beginnings.

Lois Elizabeth Allbright
San Felipe, Mexico. August 1, 2006,
Revised in Prescott, AZ, Sept 12, 2016

Addendum

Two Short Stories

The Effigy In My Closet

Originally published in *More Than Wine*, A
Collection of Stories from the Napa Valley
Scribblers Guild, 1998.

Down in Honolulu on V-J Day,
there would be dancing in the streets,
grown-ups probably doing lots of drinking
and kissing, everybody putting leis around
each other's necks. Up in Manoa, we'd
never get to see all that, unless it was on a
newsreel later. I wanted us kids to
celebrate the end of the war in our own

way. Victory over Japan was our victory too.

Mornings when I burned old newspapers, I thought about V-J Day. I tossed the *Honolulu Star Bulletin* into the incinerator, threw in the flaming match and watched the headlines that told stories about so much dying --- so many casualties here, so many there. I liked to watch those words crumple into crisp ash, then fall apart.

It was hard to imagine what Oahu would be like without barbed wire on the beaches, without sailors walking in threes so that I had to step down in the street to get around them. I didn't know if I was supposed to get mad or smile when soldiers rolling around the curbs in their jeeps wolf-whistled at me, eleven years old.

At least after V-J Day, we wouldn't have to lug around gas masks. Mine put a kink in my neck. My left hip stuck out more than the right one from balancing the darn heavy thing slung across my chest.

The best thing about V-J Day would be knowing that the Japanese weren't ever going to drop mustard gas on us. I'd rather die than strip off my clothes in the classroom in front of Robert, not to mention Takako and the other kids, and climb naked into a tub of water to get rid of the burning gas. On V-J Day, I could stop thinking about that --- one more good reason to celebrate.

As I poked the ashes with a stick, I started to sing a song that my English godmother who lived in Kaimuku taught me. It was about a fire in London a long time ago. She said that they sang the song in England on Guy Fawkes Day each year when they burned an effigy in a big bonfire. She explained that an effigy was a crude image of a hated person that was hung or burned. I pictured the fire, the doll-man hanging, the people yelling and dancing around.

That night in bed I decided to make an effigy of General Hideki Tojo. I'd seen him leering from war posters since I was eight. In the newsreels, he looked as if he had a cruel and cold heart like a human shark.

I spent some time trying out the idea of making an effigy of Emperor Hirohito, but couldn't pile up enough hate for him. After all, the Japanese worshipped their emperor, and if he had any influence with God, I wanted to be on the safe side and leave him out of my plans.

Every day or so, I added a few touches to my effigy. It made me feel strange to be doing something that my parents didn't know about. I scared myself because I discovered that I enjoyed making Tojo suffer. His effigy had bleeding wounds, broken glasses, and signs of fatal diseases. When I drew his flat nose with big nostrils, or make his eyes small and slanty, I felt a little worry in my stomach. I didn't want any of my Japanese friends to see my effigy. What if they thought I saw *them* that way!

I hid Tojo, folded up in a shoe box at the back of my closet. I could hardly wait to show him to the *haoli* neighborhood kids who had sweated through air raids with me. I gleefully imagined hanging him, then toasting him over crackling flames while we all waved American flags.

We didn't have any air raid scares for a while. General MacArthur won back the Philippines and set up a base on Okinawa. Our GIs would be invading Japan any day. After we won that battle, I'd be able to unveil my effigy.

One evening in the middle of July, 1945, I came in from playing with my friends. My parents were listening to the radio in the living room. On their faces were the same dull, shocked expressions that I had seen on December 7, 1941, when we heard the news about the attack on Pearl Harbor.

The radio was reporting that an American bomber had dropped a new kind of bomb on a Japanese city, Hiroshima. The entire city was destroyed. The people and buildings were melted into shadows by the power of the bomb.

All those deaths. I felt numb as I tried to absorb the idea that our bomb had killed mothers and fathers with their children, a whole city of them.

I sank down on the round green ottoman near my mother's chair. God would never forgive this, I was sure. The souls of those melted people were now floating above us. I imagined the sky that arched over our two countries growing dark with grief, the wind blowing the cries of Japanese babies all the way to our island, all the way into my bedroom window at night.

My parents were still listening to the radio when I carried Tojo in his box out to the incinerator. I lifted the lid of the box and took a last look at the ugly thing I'd made out of paper and an old undershirt. The crayoned tears dripping from his eyes had made me laugh a few days ago. With a choking feeling in my throat, I stuffed the box down inside the blackened oil drum. I wouldn't have to see it in my closet ever again. With my hands I scooped up piles of soft, gray ashes and let them fall over the box until it was hidden. The next morning before anyone else was up I burned it with the newspapers.

124

For The Duration

A tall man in a uniform stood
around in the gym watching us while we
sang *Over There* and my favorite, *The
Caissons Go Rolling Along,* after the Pledge
of Allegiance. Our principal, Mr. Trout,
kept all of us fifth graders who said we
wanted to be in the band sitting on a
bunch of folding chairs while the other
kids went to their homerooms. Then he

introduced the soldier. Corporal Shuckley
was going to be our band teacher.

"Corporal Shuckley is stationed
here on Oahu for the duration of the war.
He plays in the Army Band at Schofield
Barracks and will come here every
Monday to teach you music," he said. He
clapped his hands together without
making any noise.

Some of the kids raised their hands
like they might clap too, but first they
looked at Champoo, the most popular kid,
to see if he liked the idea. His black eyes
didn't say yes, or no, so we sat still waiting
for something else to happen. I thought
Mr. Trout looked disappointed. He
mumbled to us something about the war
effort and how we all have to do our part,
then walked off to his office looking
important.

"Teacher," said Ferdinand, "What instrument we get?" That started everybody talking. Corporal Shuckley grabbed a funny cardboard hat, which I found out later is a mute for a trumpet, and shook it.

"Each of you kids is going to pick a piece of paper out of this hat with the name of an instrument on it. That's the one you get to play," he said.

I got the clarinet. Ugh! I hate those squeaky black things. They've got reeds that you have to lick and change all the time. I raised my hand. "I've already decided I want a drum," I said, "so here's your paper back."

"I want it," said Champoo. So he got my clarinet and put his paper back in the hat.

Well, the hat was going around the room pretty fast, and the Corporal's neck was getting red like his khaki collar was too tight. Kids were opening instrument cases and fiddling with keys and valves. A few loud squeals from Champoo's clarinet made everybody laugh.

It probably wasn't the right time to ask for something, but I still didn't have an instrument, and not even a piece of paper. "Corporal, sir," I said, thinking that I'd better be polite. "Please may I play a drum?"

I stepped close to his shiny shoes and smiled up at him. My hair was in sausage curls just like every Monday. Most grown-ups really like that.

He looked at my Shirley Temple hair and my pink and white striped dress with puffed sleeves. I could tell that he liked it that I still had on my shoes and

socks. Most of the other kids had taken
theirs off and piled them by the door.
Staring at his belt buckle, I began to hope.

"Drum?" "What kind?" he asked,
sort of laughing.

"You know, the kind that you wear
around your neck and go rat-ta-tat-tat
with," I said.

"Snare," he said. "A snare drum?
Girls don't play snare drums."

I wanted to yell *why not*, but I
thought I'd better not argue. "I can keep
really good time when I tap on a pot with
a spoon," I said.

"That probably sounds swell in the
kitchen, but in this band I want you to
play the flute. That's more your speed.
After I get through showing Ferdinand
how to hold his trombone, I'll help you

put your flute together." He turned his back on me and walked away.

I opened the little black case and looked inside at the silver flute pieces. They were tucked into dark blue velvet slots where they fit real tight. The metal was cold and smelled oily. The places where I thought holes would be were covered with little complicated looking lids of metal on hinges. How was I going to play this thing? My fingers and knees felt weak and rubbery.

Swallowing hard, I stared at one of the forty-eight stars on the flag that was pinned to the gym wall. Ever since I knew we were going to have band, I'd been thinking about that boy in that history book picture who marches along beside the stars and stripes with the man who has a bloody rag on his head. The boy had his drum sort of slung sideways on his hip, and he looks so proud and happy with everybody marching to the sound of his drum.

The bell was going to ring, and I could see Corporal Shuckley crouched by three boys with trumpets, talking real friendly. He stood up and played a scale showing how the trumpet valves work with the keys. The notes ran up and down so light and bright that they bounced around the kids and shined on their faces.

The corporal blew some spit out the end of the trumpet and wiped his mouth with the back of his hand. He looked pretty proud of himself.

"I guess he's forgotten about me and the flute," I said to myself. "Might as well take off my shoes!"